Jo Sonja

a life in folk art

Published by:
All American Crafts, Inc.
7 Waterloo Road
Stanhope, NJ 07874
www.allamericancrafts.com

Publisher: Jerry Cohen
Chief Executive Officer: Darren Cohen
Product Development Director: Brett Cohen
Art Direction: Andy Jones
Editorial Advisor: Peggy Harris, Linda Heller,
Arlene Linton
Special thanks to: Mark Jansen and Geoffery LaLonde

All dimensions throughout the book are in inches.

Images provided by Jo Sonjas, Inc, used with permission, all rights reserved.

THE NATIONAL MUSEUM OF DECORATIVE PAINTING
1406 WOODMONT LANE
ATLANTA, GA 30318
404-351-1151
DPMUSEUM.ORG

Printed in China
©2012 National Museum of Decorative Painting
ISBN 978-1-936708-12-3
Library of Congress Control Number 2011918565

Jo Sonja

a life in folk art

Presented by the National Museum of Decorative Painting

Contents

An Expression of Joy

The title of Jo Sonja's first series of books, *An Expression of Joy*, is certainly one of the best descriptions for the work of an artist who has spent most of her life studying and sharing her love and passion for folk art. Now, after an artistic career that has encompassed over 45 years of painting, teaching, and designing, the description is still just as appropriate as it was when she first published those books in 1974.

Jo Sonja Fandrem was born in the rural Pacific Northwest and raised next to her grandparent's farm. She spent her early years surrounded by the traditions and folklore of her Scandinavian heritage. In 1957, at the tender age of 19, she and Jerry Jansen married. Then followed graduation from Sacred Heart nursing school, three children, and college — years too busy with just plain living to devote much time to painting. In the mid-1960's, children Mark, David, and Cheryl began school. As time became available, her interest in art revived, this time in the area of folk and decorative art.

Many people believe a folk artist to be an untutored artist, and Jo Sonja can fit into this description as well. Except for one and a half years of work under a very skilled decorative artist, she is primarily self-taught, beginning with sketching in childhood and continuing through oil painting in her teens, when she won her first art contest. Interest in the Norwegian heritage of her father, Pennsylvania Dutch, English, and a bit of Spanish from her mother fused with the painting desire, and folk art became her passion and an expression that refused to be denied.

As with many who began to teach and study traditional techniques in the 60's and 70's, it was extremely difficult to find resource materials. Rather than frustrate, this only served to fuel her interest and desire to keep the old traditions alive. The kind considerations of friends, neighbors, museums, and fellow artists have all combined over the many years to the gathering of knowledge that provided her inspirational foundation.

From the beginning, Jo Sonja and her husband Jerry believed in an equal partnership in marriage. They had each taken turns supporting the other while each pursued their educations. In 1975 Jerry decided to retire from his successful management career with the Southern Pacific Railroad. Feeling that he had achieved his goals, he turned his attention to supporting her efforts to pursue hers. An inseparable painting partnership was formed with Jo Sonja as the artistic inspiration and Jerry as her constant support system. Together they have traveled the world studying and teaching, published 66 instructional books, filmed instructional videos and DVDs, produced the *Artist's Journal* quarterly magazine, and much more.

By the late 1970's, Jo Sonja began to develop sensitivity to the oil media that she was using. It was obvious that this would begin limiting her opportunity to spend time painting. Unwilling to succumb to the obstacle, she sought out other options and worked closely with Wally Raley in the development of Delta Ceramcoat acrylic paints for decorative painting. New techniques had to be learned and old skills adjusted, but she made the change and transitioned her painting and teaching to the new medium. This marked the first time acrylics had been widely introduced in decorative painting. Her search for an acrylic paint that could perform to the same standards as the oils with which she had first learned and loved ultimately led to her joining forces with Jim

Folk Artist: One who finds sheer joy in painting simple straightforward decorations in rich and beautiful colors. — Jo Sonja Jansen

Cobb of Chroma Acrylics in 1983 to develop the product line of acrylic gouache that still bears her name.

Prolific in scope, her work is truly international and has appeared in cities, museums, and homes around the world, everywhere from the White House and Smithsonian to "mom's" kitchen.

In 1974, she was awarded the prestigious Master Teacher's Certificate by the National Society of Tole and Decorative Painters. In 1980, the Silver Palette award was bestowed by the same organization in recognition of her outstanding contribution to the advancement of decorative painting. In 1982, President and Mrs. Reagan selected two of her works for their White House collection. In 1996, the Vesterheim Gold Medal (VGM), honoring excellence in Rosemaling, from the Norwegian American Museum in Decorah, Iowa, became a treasured reality. In 2007, the Society of Decorative Painters awarded her the President's Commendation for noteworthy contributions of an exceptional nature.

Jo Sonja Jansen is a folk artist and teacher by first love and choice. As a folk artist, she prefers impressionism to realism and believes a certain amount of individual style in technique is more desirable than an exact copy of an existing setup. In her words, "We study the old techniques to gain an understanding and an appreciation. This knowledge allows us to develop in new individual ways and yet retain the flavor and charm of the old." While any artist's works can be naive, skill development is necessary before strong personal styles can emerge, and Jo Sonja has spent untold thousands of hours honing her skills and defining her own recognizable style. She has also spent untold thousands of hours giving back, teaching those skills, and encouraging others to develop their own individual styles in order to further their own artistic endeavors.

As you peruse the examples of her work throughout the years, it becomes apparent that her desire to study, paint, and contribute is insatiable. From the beginning in the 1960's, the scope of her work is immense and yet you can almost always see her own personal style within each of the many styles that she has painted. In one of her books, she describes her work as follows:

"Those of us who are concerned with the viability of our art form realize that the development of individuality is imperative, with respect for our traditional heritage and concern for individual self-expression. Please understand that these represent my style as it has developed from my studies with the wish that they might be of some help to you as you search for your style of self-expression."

Today, Jo Sonja Jansen continues to live in the charming, Northern California coastal town of Eureka, surrounded by the love and assistance of family and good friends — husband Jerry, son Mark, daughter-in-law Valerie, Bill and Billie Colley, and Geoff Lalonde.

She has definitely succeeded in the search for her own style of self-expression — a style that is easily recognizable as "Jo Sonja" and truly her Expression of Joy.

Jo Sonja Jansen
A Living Treasure

In 2011, Jo Sonja Jansen was proclaimed to be *A LIVING TREASURE* by the National Museum of Decorative Painting (Atlanta, Georgia) in recognition of her exceptional talents, educational contributions, and preservation of decorative painting.

As such, she is deemed to be a true creator, whose work shines brightly as a standard for this and future generations of practitioners of the art form and is invested with the mission to ensure that this invaluable heritage is passed on so that its techniques are renewed and forever reinvented.

Orange Hindeloopen Table
Acrylic gouache on wood
30 diameter x 29
1995
Collection of Mark Jansen

9

Forward

There are few decorative artists whose work is so distinctive that, with only a glance, a piece of work can be instantly attributed to them. Such is the case with renowned artist and designer Jo Sonja Jansen.

As director of the National Museum of Decorative Painting, it has been my pleasure and privilege to have known Jo Sonja for many years. Her enthusiasm for this art form knows no bounds.

She is a prolific artist who not only creates magnificent pieces of folk art, but also readily and joyfully shares her knowledge about folk art, methodology, and technique with anyone willing to listen and learn. Her desire to see this art form grow, expand, and flourish is always present.

In the year preparing for this exhibition and catalog, it has been rewarding to see her graciousness shine through. No request was too great — no deadline unmanageable.

As you look through the pages of this catalog, you will no doubt be impressed with the scope of her repertoire, her distinctive style that shines through each piece she paints, and the love she has for creating these pieces.

I hope you will be inspired by her creations, feel her joy, and be moved to study and to learn from her.

It is my pleasure to present to you, *Jo Sonja — a life in folk art.*

Andy B. Jones, Director
National Museum of Decorative Painting

Gardens of Gold
Acrylic gouache on wood
6 x 6 x 7
2007
Collection of the artist

Floral Paintings

Folk painters throughout the world have long painted floral motifs. Sometimes a certain flower was used to teach a lesson based on the symbolic meaning of the flower. Roses represented love and purity, chrysanthemums wealth and cheerfulness. Daffodils implied chivalry and respect, while daisies depicted purity and simplicity.

Often, folk art flowers reflect the natural world of the artist's homeland, but frequently they are imaginary or highly stylized motifs.

"Studying old folk art pieces prompted my first steps into stylistic flowers, and this wonderful challenge still interests me today. When you are released from the slavish need to realistically copy a flower, your heart can seek to capture the essence of the flower stylistically. This is not an easy quest, but it can be so satisfying!

I have always said, 'Folk art is the cradle of impressionism.' A true sense of completion comes over me when I read or hear some other individual confirm this belief with their personal observations and studied viewpoints." — Jo Sonja

Vintage Florals
Acrylic gouache on wood
9 ½ x 7 ½ x 8
2008
Collection of the artist

13

Floral Hours
Acrylic gouache on wood
16 diameter
2008
Collection of the artist

Secret Garden of the White Rabbit
Acrylic gouache on wood
20 diameter
2008
Collection of the artist

Midsummer's Morn
Acrylic gouache on wood
16 diameter
2001
Collection of the artist

Bowl of Roses
Acrylic gouache on tin
14 ½ diameter
2007
Collection of the artist

Garden of the Golden Phœnix
Acrylic gouache on wood
8 ½ x 6 ½ x 4 ¼
2011
Collection of the artist

Vintage Floral Vase
Acrylic gouache on wood
13 x 10 x 3 ½
2010
Collection of the artist

Vintage Moonlight Tray
Acrylic gouache on tin
20 diameter
2000
Private collection

Black Swan
Acrylic on wood
29 x 10 x 20
1983
Collection of the artist

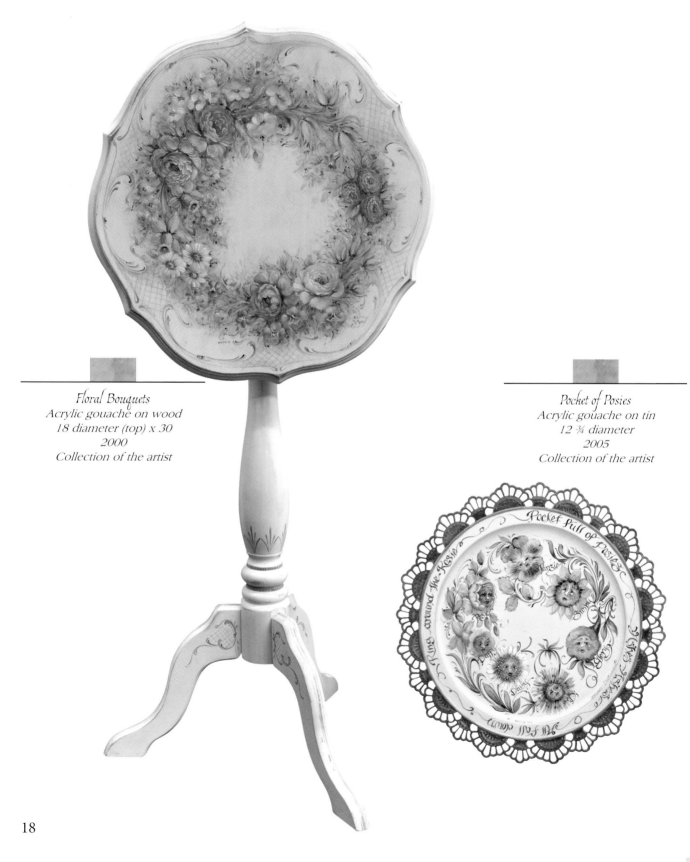

Floral Bouquets
Acrylic gouache on wood
18 diameter (top) x 30
2000
Collection of the artist

Pocket of Posies
Acrylic gouache on tin
12 ¾ diameter
2005
Collection of the artist

18

Pearlescent Florals
Acrylic gouache on wood
18 diameter
2006
Collection of the artist

Pansy Thoughts
Acrylic gouache on wood
4 ¾ x 4 ¾ x 4 ½
2011
Collection of the artist

19

Blended Florals
Acrylic gouache on paper
9 x 12
1996
Collection of the artist

The Painted Rose Blooms All Year
Acrylic gouache on wood
16 x 12 x 10
2008
Collection of the National
Museum of Decorative Painting

Folk Figures

Even before the glorious realism of classical antiquity, the desire to capture the human form has been pursued by artisans and craftsmen. The folk artist is no different.

Creating a representative likeness of a human form and placing the figure in a narrative to tell a story is central to many works of folk art. Illustrated stories have been painted on walls, panels, and furnishings for centuries by folk artists who have drawn on a wealth of historic inspiration to paint their own unique version of the human figure.

"The abundant old folk art pieces decorated with these figures have been a source of wonderful inspiration for me. Working figures into a design, stylizing the figures to make them decorative, and placing them at the desired point of interest in designs has become a fascinating challenge.

This presentation of the decorative figure versus the realistic figure continues to give me hours of painting pleasure." — Jo Sonja

Bowl with Maiden
In loving memory of my mother
Acrylic gouache on wood
Carving by Tim Montzka
20 diameter
1993
Collection of the artist

23

Immigrant's Wedding Stien
Oil on wood
8 ½ x 13 ½
1976
Collection of the artist

Peasant Folk
Oil on wood
17 x 13
1975
Collection of the artist

The Flower Vendor
Oil on canvas
16 x 20
1975
Collection of the artist

Thomas J's Evening Pipe
Acrylic gouache on wood
5 ¾ x 4 x 18 ½
1985
Collection of the artist

The Village of Crumb
Oil on wood
40 x 24 x 29
1978
Collection of Mark Jansen

Grapestompers Hutch
Oil on wood
66 x 21 x 81 ½
1980
Collection of the artist

Under the Apple Tree
Acrylic gouache on wood
12 diameter
2008
Collection of the artist

Apple Tree Jelly Cupboard
Acrylic on wood
62 x 18 ¾ x 11
1980
Private collection

28

Linen Cupboard
Acrylic gouache on wood
26 ¼ x 18 x 62 ¼
1991
Collection of the artist

To Love & To Cherish
Acrylic gouache on paper
12 x 9
1985
Collection of the artist

The Immigrants
Acrylic on canvas
16 x 16
1985
Collection of the artist

Sewers
Acrylic on canvas
14 x 11
1985
Collection of the artist

31

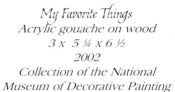

Good Wishes
Acrylic gouache on metal
12 x 12
1996
Private collection

My Favorite Things
Acrylic gouache on wood
3 x 5 ¼ x 6 ½
2002
Collection of the National
Museum of Decorative Painting

Thee I Love
Acrylic gouache on wood
20 x 13 ½ x 4 ½
1986
Collection of the artist

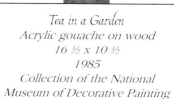

Tea in a Garden
Acrylic gouache on wood
16 ½ x 10 ½
1985
Collection of the National
Museum of Decorative Painting

From the Italian Alps
Oil on wood
16 diameter
1979
Collection of the artist

In the Italian Alps
Oil on wood
21 x 12 x 2
1974
Collection of the artist

Sing a Song of Sixpence
Acrylic gouache on tin
16 ½ x 10 ½
2008
Collection of the artist

The Fruited Branch
Acrylic gouache on tin
10 ½ x 8 x 9
2005
Collection of the artist

Adam's Rib
Acrylic gouache on wood
18 diameter
2003
Private collection

Harlequin Nutcracker
Acrylic gouache on metal
12 x 7
1997
Private collection

The Pirates of Dolphin Cove
Acrylic gouache on wood
8 ½ x 11 ½ x 7 ¼
2010
Collection of the artist

Black Joe La Trump & Jingles
Acrylic gouache on wood
15 ¾ x 10 ¼ x 11 ¾
2006
Collection of Mark Jansen

Tole Strokes
Acrylic gouache on metal
10 x 8 ½ x 6
2008
Collection of the National
Museum of Decorative Painting

Earth Angel
Acrylic gouache on resin
7 x 18 x 4
2010
Collection of the National
Museum of Decorative Painting

Sweet Mary
Acrylic gouache on tin
11 diameter
1995
Private collection

Study in the style of
Johann Michæl Röfsler
Acrylic gouache on wood
13 x 6 x 15 ½
2008
Collection of the artist

Religious Themes

Historically, religion has provided common themes, lessons, and stories to all manner of artists. Christianity indelibly left its mark on western art. This imagery and iconography has also been the inspiration for countless folk artists.

The holy family, saints, angels, figures, and stories from the Bible have provided a wealth of subject matter for the folk artist. These elements were often combined with secular motifs for pictorial variety and are found on both devotional and everyday objects.

Whether depicting a nativity scene, Biblical story, or even a moral lesson, the folk artist has always, and will always, find vast inspiration from their religious beliefs.

"My mother once asked if I remembered to thank God for painting's gifts and opportunities. Hugging her, I replied 'Mother, that is what this is all about.'

Painting religious-themed works provides a special time of worship and praise in my life. I remember painting *The Good Shepherd* bowl and how it just wonderfully happened as I lost all sense of time. Too quickly the painting of the scene was completed and I truly don't remember it taking more than a moment. It was a very blessed moment." — Jo Sonja

*Chest of the St. Nikolas Fraternity
of the Inn Sailors
Acrylic gouache on wood
11 x 6 x 8 ¼
2008
Collection of the artist*

41

Madonna and Child
Acrylic gouache, gold leaf on paper
11 x 9
1996
Collection of the artist

The Good Shepherd
Acrylic gouache on wood
16 diameter
1995
Collection of the artist

Adam & Eve
Acrylic gouache on wood
Carving by Tim Montzka
18 ¼ diameter
1995
Collection of Mark Jansen

Renaissance Bench
Acrylic on wood
20 x 15 x 26
1979
Private collection

Illuminated Manuscripts Triptych
Acrylic gouache on wood
18 x 20 x 3 ¼
2004
Collection of the artist

Out of Egypt
Acrylic gouache on paper
9 x 12
1985
Collection of the artist

Folk Art Styles

Folk art is as varied as the regions and eras from which it springs. Never a static art form, it also reflects influences from other cultures and artists with which it comes in contact. The result is hundreds upon hundreds of unique styles.

"The following section of this book will showcase some of my favorite styles and should give you an overview of what is possible when you open your heart and palette to the glorious tradition of folk art from around the world.

It is interesting to see how there are universal themes and motifs which run through so many folk art styles (flowers, leaf forms, birds, etc.), and to see how each culture or region interprets them so uniquely.

When studying any painting style, I think it is important to study the entire culture — from song and dance to costume and home. The art of the common people reflects their whole culture and lifestyle.

If I wish to paint a style, I must enjoy the whole atmosphere of the culture. This has been the most rewarding aspect of my folk art journey: to 'visit' with others through their cultural mores and folk customs."
— Jo Sonja

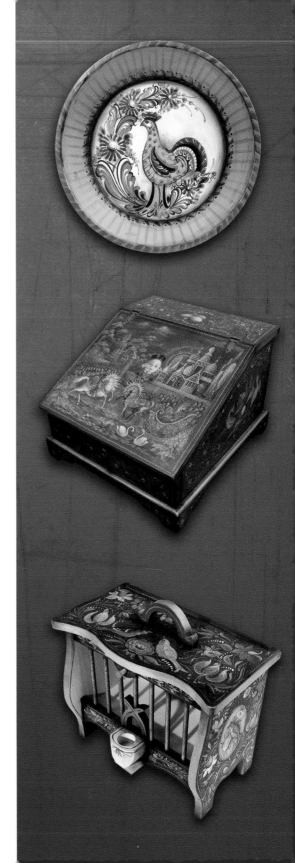

Swedish

Chippendale

Rosemaling

Russian

Appenzell

French Bridal Painting

Austrian & German

Narrow Boat Painting

Swedish

Although there are different Swedish styles, often developed through the preferences of a certain area, the paintings of the central province of Dalarna are perhaps the best known. Often simply referred to as "Dala" painting, it was historically painted with distemper paint. Simple folk scenes are often embellished with large fountains of stylized flowers, leaves, and gourds. These distinctive gourd trees were inspired by the Bible story of Jonah, who, falling asleep in the hot sun, was provided shade when God caused a gourd tree to grow over him.

"Dala wall paintings are on light backgrounds and the furniture is darker with stylized gourd trees, usually framed with Kleister techniques. The decorative effect of the furniture against the lighter decorated walls is visually stunning.

Sometimes I like to take the wall painting techniques and decorate a lighter-colored piece with my own interpretation of the style. This is not a violation of the old heritage, as I have seen lighter pieces in Sweden. I do like to use different themes, as illustrated by the Dala clock decorated with stylized illustrations of the fairy tale, *Sleeping Beauty*." — Jo Sonja

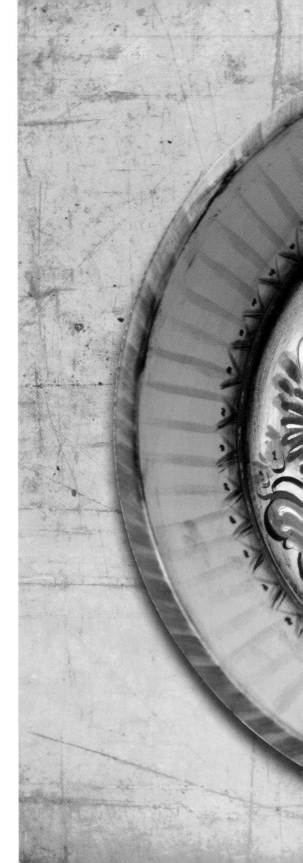

Swedish Cockerel
Acrylic gouache on tin
9 x 2
2007
Collection of the artist

49

Garden Welcome
Acrylic gouache on wood
14 ½ x 19 ¾
2005
Collection of the artist

Swedish Dala Clock
Acrylic gouache on wood
27 x 10 x 7
2002
Collection of the artist

Swedish Briar Rose
Acrylic gouache on wood
20 diameter
2002
Collection of the artist

Memories of Rattvick
Acrylic gouache on wood
16 x 12 x 10
2008
Collection of Crayola LLC

Chippendale

English tin and papier-mâché pieces decorated with golden scrolls, varied scenes, stylized flowers, and birds are usually called japanned, or Chippendale decorated wares. Gold leaf and mother-of-pearl inlays are also included in the decoration of some of the more elaborate pieces. Although the painted pieces may use his name, celebrated furniture maker Thomas Chippendale did not originate this style of decoration.

The Chippendale technique assumes depth and dimension through the use of white underpainting with transparent overstrokes (a layering technique that also provided the inspiration for Russian Zhostova painting). Many pieces utilize a black, or dark, background that enhances the vibrant colors of the often very ornate design work.

"Underpainting sometimes with color, transparent Kleister strokes, and tinting with transparent colors are some of my favorite techniques and I include them often in my work. Developing my own themes and stylized objects has been a delightful challenge and the techniques lend a unique look to many of my paintings." — Jo Sonja

Victoria's Garden
Acrylic gouache on metal
20 ½ x 17
2003
Collection of the artist

53

Coral Branches
Acrylic gouache on metal
21 ¼ x 17 ½
2006
Collection of the artist

Peacock Fountain
Acrylic gouache on metal
20 ¼ x 16
2005
Collection of the artist

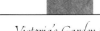

Victoria's Garden Clock
Acrylic gouache on wood
16 x 12 x 10
2008
Collection of Mark Jansen

The Garden of the Peacock
Acrylic gouache on metal
20 ½ x 17
2005
Collection of the artist

Rosemaling

"*Growing* up in a small valley area just south of Springfield, Oregon, we lived at the edge of my paternal grandparents farm. This area was home to many immigrant relatives from Norway and influenced my early years; however, we did not speak the Norwegian language because, as my grandfather said, 'We are Americans.'

Interestingly, I was not really aware of Norwegian rosemaling until I took my first tole painting classes at the adult education center in Eugene, where I met Gudrun Berg, an immigrant from Norway. Gudrun had brought with her some pieces of Os rosemaling that we thoroughly studied. This style was not yet given a name, so we called it west coast rosemaling, meaning the west coast of Norway, not the United States. Our research on rosemaling styles led to contacts with Vesterheim (the Norwegian American museum in Decorah, Iowa) and other early rosemalers. So began my fusion of heritage and folk art.

Norway has a great history of various folk art styles, and Nils Ellingsgard has been a leader in this research. I've been very fortunate to study with many Norwegian and American rosemalers and especially thank Nils for his help when seeking to improve my technique using acrylics." — Jo Sonja

Heritage Legacy Bowl
Acrylic gouache on wood
Carving by Hans Sondom
22 ½ x 15 ½ x 6
1992
Collection of the artist

Hallingdal

"*Large* stylized flowers, simple scrolls, a wealth of scenes, people, and animals make this a fun style to present. Vibrant colors, strong contrast, and a simple palette make for a very good decorative presentation. Textured work is further enhanced with antiquing techniques.

This style was frequently taught by Nils Ellingsgard, a third-generation artist from the area. Jerry and I are very lucky to have a piece painted by Nil's grandfather in our collection. I am also fond of pieces by Amund Myro that remind me of Hawaiian leis with their strings of flowers." — Jo Sonja

Hallingdal Tine
Acrylic gouache on wood
11 ¼ x 9 ¾ x 6
2008
Collection of the artist

Rococo

"*Rococo* is an extension of the architecturally influenced style of decoration found in almost all European communities. Based on oval shapes, this style usually features scroll designs. The scrolls are delicate and many times do not touch each other, but are joined with shell-like details. Light, airy, and usually more refined than other styles, rococo brings a refreshing openness to scroll painting.

Ragnavald Froysdal presented a heavier rococo style with great variation. It was fun to study with him." — Jo Sonja

Rococo Rosemaling Bowl
Acrylic gouache on wood
16 diameter
2008
Collection of the artist

Rogaland

"*Rogaland* is from the southwest coastal region of Norway. Flowers are more important and more predominant than scrolls and leaves, with tulips, stylized roses, four and six-petal flowers, daisies, and stylized lilies commonly portrayed. The designs are symmetrical, generally utilizing opaque colors and typically feature crosshatching, dots, and teardrops.

Most often, Rogland is painted on darker backgrounds, but I think medium and lighter value backgrounds can make for vibrant and interesting paintings — this is how styles grow, change and evolve." — Jo Sonja

Rogaland Pie Basket
Acrylic gouache on wood
12 x 12 x 3
2010
Collection of the artist

Rosemaling in the Round
Acrylic gouache on wood
12 x 9 ¾
2000
Collection of the artist

61

Os

"*The* Os style remains a favorite of mine, as it reminds me of a delightful, casual collection of wildflowers. Fresh, open, airy collections of stylized flowers and leaves spread their colors and freshness of spirit across many wooden surfaces.

I prefer to keep this style very casual and not overworked or too fussy. Strokes, double loading, tipping, etc., are just a few of the technical possibilities of this style. Buildings, people, and animals can also be included, giving this style wonderful design possibilities." — Jo Sonja

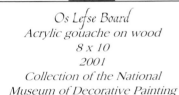

Os Lefse Board
Acrylic gouache on wood
8 x 10
2001
Collection of the National
Museum of Decorative Painting

Os Tray
Acrylic gouache on wood
20 x 10 ½
2006
Collection of the artist

Vest Agder

"*From* the most southern area of Norway, this style is refreshing in its simplicity with strong contrasts and a simple color palette. True, later examples became very fussy and, to some people, overdone, but we must say 'to each his own.'

Flat-bottomed tulips, scrolls that look like palm trees, and pineapple plants fire my imagination with new inspiration. This is the area where we find many paintings of the wedding procession, even a few drunks, and other individuals of the community." — Jo Sonja

Vest Agder Baroque Vase
Acrylic gouache on wood
16 ¼ x 11 x 3
2008
Collection of the artist

Vest Agder Sewing Box
Acrylic gouache on wood
14 x 9 x 5 ¾
2007
Collection of the artist

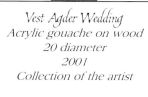

Vest Agder Wedding Portrait
Acrylic gouache on wood
20 diameter
2001
Collection of the artist

Vest Agder Wedding
Acrylic gouache on wood
20 diameter
2001
Collection of the artist

Telemark

"*This* style is scroll painting with small flower embellishments. There are many individual artist variations, giving opportunity for hours of pleasurable study. Here again, I prefer the beauty and power of the more casual stroke presentations.

I have been indeed fortunate to have the opportunity to study with Sigmund Aarseth, observe him paint, and watch his work change over the years." — Jo Sonja

Rosemaling by an Immigrant's
Granddaughter - Telemark Style
Acrylic gouache on wood
13 ½ x 8 ¾ x 7 ¼
2009
Collection of the artist

Telemark Cabinet
Acrylic gouache on wood
17 x 28 x 7 ½
2003
Collection of the artist

Heritage Telemark Tine
Acrylic gouache on wood
17 x 10 ½ x 8
1996
Collection of the artist

Telemark Sleigh Ride
Acrylic gouache on wood
14 ½ x 11 ¾
1996
Collection of Mark Jansen

Dry Brush Telemark Tine
Acrylic gouache on wood
10 ½ x 6
1991
Collection of the artist

Personal Style

In the book *Norwegian Folk Art – The Migration of a Tradition*, Dr. Marion Nelson, former director of the Vesterheim Norwegian-American Museum in Decorah, Iowa, describes Jo Sonja Jansen's work this way:

"Her forte is creating designs with total disregard for regional consistency that get their unity through what she brings to them. Her wedding bowl (pictured on page 57), based on her personal mythology of marriage, masterfully brings medieval dragons, Hallingdal flowers, acanthus carving, and products of her own imagination into a remarkably consistent artistic statement. It is an example of totally digested heritage and is a truly folk creation executed by an individual of extreme technical and aesthetic sophistication."

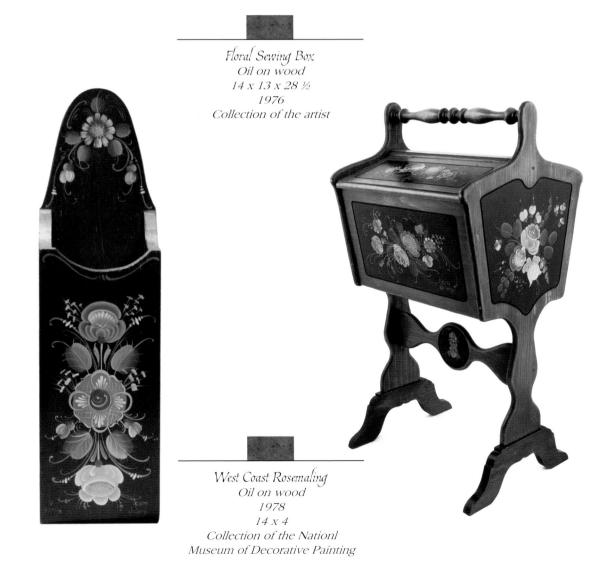

Floral Sewing Box
Oil on wood
14 x 13 x 28 ½
1976
Collection of the artist

West Coast Rosemaling
Oil on wood
1978
14 x 4
Collection of the Nationl
Museum of Decorative Painting

The Setesdal Rose
Acrylic gouache on wood
12 ½ x 7 ¾ x 9 ½
2011
Collection of the artist

Genesis Bowl
Acrylic gouache on wood
20 ½ x 3
1997
Collection of Vesterheim
Norwegian-American Museum
Decorah, Iowa

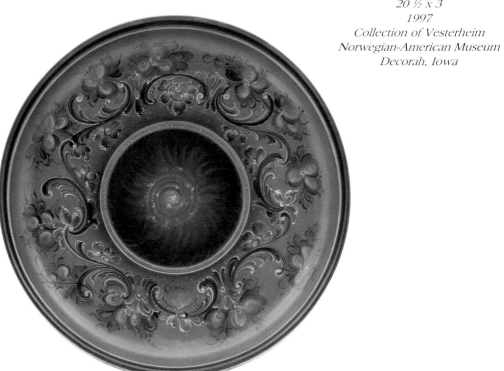

Norwegian Life Tapestry Tine
Acrylic gouache on wood
12 x 9 ½ x 6 ½
1994
Collection of the artist

Winter Rose of Telemark Porringer
40th Wedding Anniversary
Celebration
Acrylic gouache on wood
Carving by Hans Sandom
23 x 17 ½ x 4 ½
1997
Collection of the artist

Winter Rose of Telemark Bowl
40th Wedding Anniversary
Celebration
Acrylic gouache on wood
Carving by Hans Sandom
15 x 12 x 6
1997
Collection of the artist

Russian-Inspired

Japanned miniatures with legends, fairy tales, and village life scenes, wooden toys and treenware decorated with simple stroke designs, and metal trays with beautiful rhythmic strokes of stylized flowers of glowing colors are all part of Russian paint decoration. Often, the production of these items involved entire villages.

"The use of white and pale-colored under painting, glazes, and stroke presentation are part of this tradition. The nobility sent their serfs to learn floral painting techniques in France. Returning to long Russian winters and darker homes, they adapted the techniques using more intense colors to brighten their homes with jewel-like miniatures and flowers. We also must not forget the charming toys and items of daily use decorated with simpler stylized stroke designs.

The variety of Russian styles and techniques continues to encourage me in my own work. Since these styles are still painted today and provide support for many artists, I choose to support these artists, buying some of their works to share with others and continue on my own personal artistic journey, finding new ways to present the appreciation of their traditional work." — Jo Sonja

Humpski Dumpski
Acrylic gouache on wood
13 x 12 x 8 ¾
1992
Collection of Mark Jansen

For Mother
Acrylic gouache on wood
10 diameter
1986
Private collection

The Dairy
Acrylic gouache on wood
12 diameter
1986
Private collection

The Little Mermaid
Acrylic gouache on wood
8 ½ x 7 ¼ x 8
1987
Collection of Mark Jansen

Russian Stroke Floral
Acrylic gouache on metal
12 diameter
1985
Private collection

Snow Queen Sleigh
Acrylic gouache on wood
10 x 17 x 29
1985
Private collection

Zhostova Style Floral Table
Acrylic gouache on wood
16 x 12 x 10
2008
Collection of the Mark Jansen

Sleigh Ride
Acrylic gouache on wood
7 ½ x 10 ¼ x 3 ¾
1987
Collection of the artist

Appenzell

The unique form of Swiss Appenzell, or herd painting, originated among Alpine dairy farmers who carved and painted farm implements as far back as the early eighteenth century. There are several typical forms including wooden pails with decorated bases, long boards or paper strips picturing cattle drives to the high Alpine pastures, and shutters with large-scale paintings of cowherders.

Cowherd art is more of an individual folk art presentation within the traditional themes. There have been numerous artists painting scenes of everyday life decorated with stylized flowers. Each artist has his/her own style that can be identified by knowledgeable researchers or collectors.

"Trudging up a hill to a private studio, Jerry and I finally found one piece of cowherd art for sale. The delightful small, thin circle of wood was $6,000 – a bit expensive for us, and this was 20 years ago. This certainly illustrates the potential value of our art, especially when we can develop our own style and create individual paintings.

These paintings reveal the value of naive works (works of unaffected simplicity). It is this very naiveté that makes the work or piece of art so valuable. What is the lesson to me? Create happily, unaffected by rules. Present what my heart wants to say!"
— Jo Sonja

Appenzell Summer
Acrylic gouache on wood
13 x 7 x 6
2007
Collection of the artist

The Alpfahrt
Acrylic gouache on wood
11 x 15 ¾
2008
Collection of the artist

Appenzell Folk Art
Acrylic gouache on wood
10 ¾ x 4
2006
Collection of the artist

French Bridal Painting

French bridal painting is a beautiful style that evolved from the decoration of small items from the Alsace-Lorraine area and Northern Switzerland. Flower patterns spread out over the background, often black, much as on a carpet or tapestry. Love symbols such as hearts and paired birds abound.

"I became aware of this style through the book *The Art of Painted Furniture* by Dr. Gislind Ritz, in the early 70's and I have always sought more information on these colorful pieces.

This style has been evolving since the love boxes of the early middle ages and has influenced the styles of nearby areas. Dutch decorative artist Jacque Zuidema decorated small items for a French winery to present their wines and candies. He brought to this style his own interpretation of the Dutch Assendelft flower style and really inspired a renewed interest and interpretation of this highly decorative style.

I particularly enjoy its more simple and refreshing stroke presentation featuring tipping and sideloading techniques that encourage 'a la fresca' work. This is a style to make your heart sing!" — Jo Sonja

French Bridal Birdcage
Acrylic gouache on wood
11 x 6 x 8 ½
2008
Collection of the artist

French Bridal Celebration
Acrylic gouache on paper
12 x 9
2008
Collection of the artist

Anniversary Clock
Acrylic gouache on wood
16 x 12 x 10
2008
Collection of the National
Museum of Decorative Painting

French Bridal Cache
Acrylic gouache on wood
9 ½ x 7 ½ x 7 ½
2008
Collection of the artist

89

Austrian & German

This term designates hundreds of styles —
from naive works to guild-influenced
pieces of great complexity. Faux finishes,
textures, and a variety of themes and
techniques are featured.

"Such examples have encouraged me
to experiment and bring more variety to
my work. Seeing the changes in artistic
presentation as styles in decoration
evolved encourages me to be more aware
of current colors and styles and relate my
work to the changes as needed. Of course,
traditional studies are always appropriate,
especially if one gives them an antique finish
and presentation.

Thankfully many countries are very
conscious of the tourist appeal their
museums have to those of us who wish to
study their folk art, and we can see many
fine examples of decorative art within their
walls. One may also take advantage of study
tours presented by select individuals and
museum groups.

The bottom line, however, is to be true to
your own vision and stay true to your own
sense of decoration in relationship to current
architectural styles and trends. If you find that
you are 'stuck in a rut,' still doing what you
did years ago, perhaps you need a little
new inspiration." — Jo Sonja

Flaming Tulip Chest
Madonna & Christ Child
Acrylic gouache on wood
29 ½ x 18 x 20 ½
1991
Collection of Mark Jansen

Flaming Tulip Chest
Madonna & Christ Child
detail
Acrylic gouache on wood
29 ½ x 18 x 20 ½
1991
Collection of Mark Jansen

Austrian Courtship
Acrylic gouache on wood
30 x 23 x 13
1991
Collection of the artist

Narrow Boat Painting

Narrow boats transported goods on the waterways or canals of England. By the 1800's, it was fairly common to see painted roses and castles on both narrow boats themselves and their fixtures and fittings. The most common areas for decoration include the doors to the cabin, the water can or barrel, and the side of the boat, along with ornate lettering stating the boat's name and owner.

"Many families lived on these boats, enriching their lives with decorative painting both inside the cabin and on the outside of the boat. The simplicity of the style is easily understandable when we realize that the decoration was to be viewed from a distance (unless you wish to fall into the canal). Fussy detailed work could not be appreciated.

This style also illustrates the value of linear decoration and lettering in combination with scenes and flowers. English narrow boat painting has opened a new appreciation for the importance of combining lines and shapes in a design. These wonderful examples have encouraged me to be more simple and direct in my decorative stroke techniques."
— Jo Sonja

94

Canal Boat Tray
Acrylic gouache on tin
16 ½ x 10 ½
1983
Private collection

Canal Boat Buckby
Acrylic on tin
10 x 12
1983
Collection of the artist

Canal Boat Inspiration Clock
Acrylic gouache on wood
66 x 15 x 9
1987
Collection of the artist

Whimsical Animals

Some of the earliest representations of animals can be found on the walls of caves in France and Spain painted some 32,000 years ago. Through the ensuing eons, animals have continued to be a favorite subject of folk artists the world over.

Often animals are depicted in a rather naïve, highly stylized form, recognizable only by shape. Other times, the artists take great liberties with color and pattern.

One of the most charming aspects of animals in folk painting is their personality. Often ferocious animals, such as lions or dragons, are portrayed with very humorous or gentle personalities! It doesn't matter whether the animal depicted is a regal horse or eagle or a lowly cow or pig, as any animal is suitable material for an imaginative folk painter.

"As a little girl, I lived on a farm and didn't have human friends until I started grade school. I played with animals, dressed them, invited them to my tea parties, and enjoyed their companionship. When I began painting, it was very natural to invite them into my personal painting expression. I have relived many happy memories as these animals have reentered my life through my paintings." — Jo Sonja

Noah's 2 x 2
Acrylic gouache on wood
20 diameter
2001
Collection of Mark Jansen

Playtime
Acrylic on canvas
16 x 20
1983
Collection of the artist

Babon's Bait Bucket
Acrylic on tin
9 x 6 x 6 ½
1984
Collection of the artist

The Nestlings - Chickens
Oil on masonite
17 ½ x 21
1975
Collection of the artist

The Nestlings - Ducks
Oil on masonite
17 ½ x 21
1975
Collection of the artist

Matilda
Oil on wood
32 ½ x 14
1974
Collection of the artist

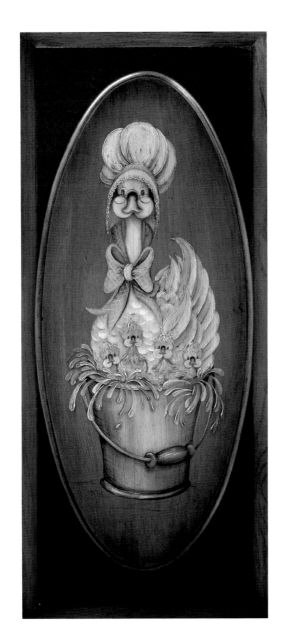

Sugar Lips & Gillipin
Oil on wood
18 diameter
1976
Collection of the artist

Chanticleer & Partlett
Acrylic gouache on wood
11 diameter
1986
Collection of the artist

White Rooster - Textured Stroke
Florals
Acrylic gouache on wood
16 diameter
1996
Collection of the artist

103

Tales of the Sea
Acrylic gouache on wood
11 ½ x 4
2000
Collection of the artist

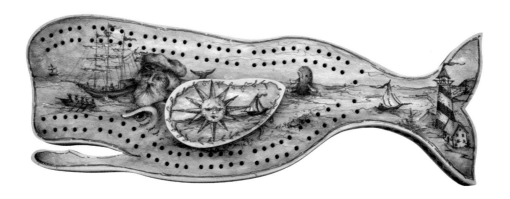

Whale Cribbage Board
Acrylic gouache on wood
12 ½ x 5
1992
Collection of the artist

Red Summer
Acrylic gouache on wood
15 ½ diameter
1996
Collection of the artist

The Bunny Renaissance
Acrylic gouache on wood
12 diameter
1985
Private collection

Hip Hop's Veggie Garden
Acrylic gouache on tin
15 ½ x 11 x 10 ½
2001
Collection of the artist

Boar-re-gard and the Boys
Acrylic gouache on wood
29 x 23 x 12
1986
Collection of the artist

Cuthbert & Candace
Oil on wood
18 x 35 ½ x 2
1977
Collection of the artist

Folk Tales

Artists have, for centuries, translated beloved folk stories into whimsical narratives. Russian lacquer boxes illustrate their fairy tales in every imaginable form. Strange animals from Norse legends find their way into rosemaling. The richer a culture's folk story tradition, the more it finds its way into its art.

"Need a little inspiration? Read an old fairy tale or folk story and try to illustrate it. Then take that step beyond the flat surface and find the perfect dimensional piece for your inspiration. The marriage of a dimensional, useful piece, and a stylized design is one of my favorite painting experiences.

It is always exciting to hear a new folk tale or legend and think of wonderful ways that I can convey that through painting. I encourage each artist to express their own ideas and include these ideas on their piece however they wish. Over the years, students and I have had such good times together with many precious memories of wonderful hours with our brushes and color."
— Jo Sonja

Pumpkin Shell Treats & Sweets
Acrylic gouache on tin
8 ½ x 6 ½ x 8 ½
2008
Collection of the artist

Alice's Tea Party
Acrylic gouache on wood
20 diameter x 11 ½
1995
Collection of Mark Jansen

Rub-A-Dub-Dub
Acrylic gouache on tin
16 ½ x 10 ½
2010
Collection of the artist

Peter and the Wolf
Acrylic gouache on wood
16 x 11 x 12
2001
Collection of Mark Jansen

Rip Van Winkle
Acrylic gouache on wood
18 x 12 x 11
2005
Collection of Mark Jansen

The Nutcracker
Acrylic gouache on tin
13 x 9 ¼ x 10 ½
2006
Collection of Mark Jansen

Heidi Plate
Acrylic gouache on wood
20 diameter
2010
Collection of the artist

Heidi
Acrylic gouache on wood
14 ½ x 14 x 10
2009
Collection of the artist

Thumbelina
Acrylic gouache on wood
15 x 8 ¼ x 12
2009
Collection of the artist

Fruit Paintings

Over time, many fruits have developed symbolic meanings in folk art. Apples can signify wisdom or temptation, grapes often imply abundance, and cherries represent fertility or modesty.

Much like flowers, fruits have provided unlimited inspiration for the folk artist. While sometimes portrayed realistically, they have often been transposed into the highly stylized motifs often seen on old tinware — referred to as tole painting.

"My neighbor and I were in a furniture refinishing and antiquing class at the adult education center in Eugene, Oregon in the late 1960's when a woman dashed in and said that tole painting classes would be offered next term. My friend looked at me and asked, 'What is tole painting?' I replied that I didn't know, but it sounded like fun to me. It was and it still is!

The fruit paintings of Peter Ompir were inspirational to me in the early years of the revival of decorative painting. I personally love the opportunity to express gorgeous colors side-by-side. This is what initially drew me to painting fruit. Then, to place them on an old tin piece — what fun!" — Jo Sonja

Harvest Fruits
Acrylic gouache on wood
15 x 6 x 9
2006
Collection of the artist

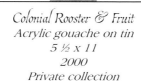

Fruit Samper
Acrylic gouaché on wood
9 ½ diameter
2000
Collection of the artist

Tole Strokes
Acrylic gouache on metal
8 ½ x 5 ½
2000
Collection of the National
Museum of Decorative Painting

Lefse Board
Acrylic gouache on wood
15 x 11 ½
1995
Collection of the National
Museum of Decorative Painting

Mountain Mary
Acrylic gouache on tin
9 ½ x 5
2004
Private collection

Harvest Fruit
Acrylic gouache on tin
10 x 8 ¾ x 9
2006
Collection of the artist

Christmas

"*Christmas* is a time of giving, a time of joy, beautiful colors at the darkest time of the year, the light of the beautiful star recaptured in a candle, a blazing fire and hot cocoa warming frosty noses and fingers, a jolly old elf with twinkling eyes and a sack of gifts.

The night is chilly as I bundle in my old wool sweater, stockings, and warm slippers and go to my paint room. All is quiet. Turning on an inspirational program or music, I open my paint palette and begin work on my yearly gift to God and the expression of His love, the Holy Child.

This is usually the time for the joyous task of painting a Christmas triptych or plate. When we were presenting the *Artist's Journal*, I loved doing the Christmas plate series most of all.

I am constantly fascinated by the abundant tales of St. Nicholas, Sinerklaus, Chris Cringle, Baboushka, Père Noël, or even La Befana! Whether I'm painting a Biblical nativity scene or drawing upon Christmas traditions from other cultures to be my inspiration, painting these pieces are the most special to me. Study, read, research, and see what wonderful yuletide creations flow from your brush!" — Jo Sonja

Santa Legends
Acrylic gouache on wood
19 x 15 x 12 ½
1994
Collection of Mark Jansen

123

Christmas Eve Traveler
Acrylic gouache on wood
10 x 11 ½
2000
Private collection

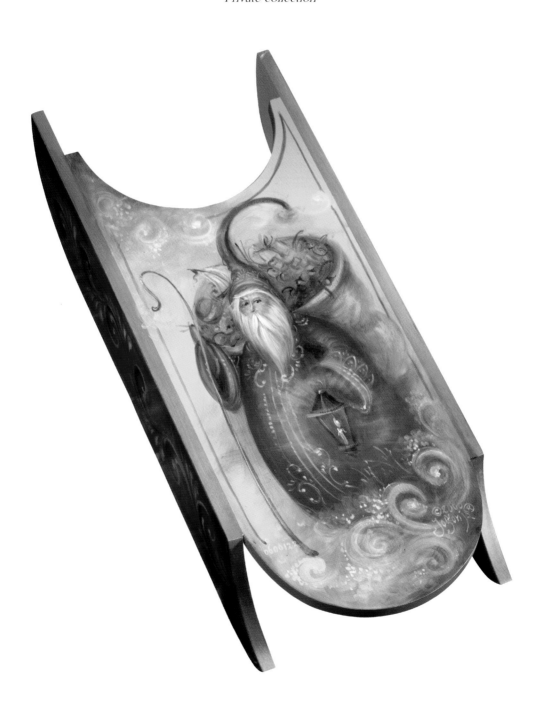

Jolly Ole Elf
Acrylic gouache on wood
20 x 10 ½ x 4 ½
1989
Private collection

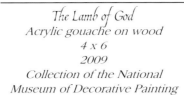

The Lamb of God
Acrylic gouache on wood
4 x 6
2009
Collection of the National
Museum of Decorative Painting

And A Partridge
Acrylic gouache on tin
16 ½ x 10 ½
2005
Collection of the artist

Nativity of the Flowers
Acrylic gouache on wood
18 diameter
2001
Collection of Mark Jansen

O Come Let Us
Adore Him
19 x 23 ¼
1987
Acrylic gouache on wood
Collection of Mark Jansen

Adoration of the Little Angels
20 ¾ x 22 ¾
1981
Acrylic gouache on wood
Collection of the National
Museum of Decorative Painting

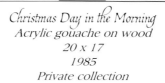

Christmas Day in the Morning
Acrylic gouache on wood
20 x 17
1985
Private collection

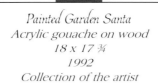

Painted Garden Santa
Acrylic gouache on wood
18 x 17 ¾
1992
Collection of the artist

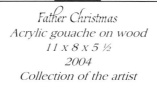

Father Christmas
Acrylic gouache on wood
11 x 8 x 5 ½
2004
Collection of the artist

O Holy Night
Acrylic gouache on wood
4 ½ x 2 ½ x 12
2008
Collection of the National
Museum of Decorative Painting

Glory

In a
Manger far away
our precious Lord and
Saviour lay.
Angels in the heavens
Sing, Praises to the
Newborn King.

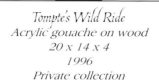

Jolly Old St. Nicholas
Acrylic gouache on wood
18 diameter
2000
Collection of Mark Jansen

Nussknacker and Mause König
The Nutcracker and Mouse King
Acrylic gouache on wood
16 diameter
1992
Collection of Mark Jansen

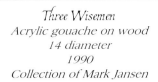

Three Wisemen
Acrylic gouache on wood
14 diameter
1990
Collection of Mark Jansen

Glory to God on Earth
Acrylic gouache on wood
16 diameter
1996
Collection of Mark Jansen

The Gingerbread Man
Acrylic gouache on wood
14 diameter
1995
Collection of Mark Jansen

Here We Come a Caroling
Acrylic gouache on wood
16 diameter
2008
Collection of Mark Jansen

O Tannenbaum
Acrylic gouache on wood
14 diameter
2008
Collection of Mark Jansen

A Little Christmas Magic
Acrylic gouache on wood
14 diameter
1991
Collection of Mark Jansen

141

Santa's Workshop
Acrylic gouache on wood
16 diameter
2010
Collection of the artist

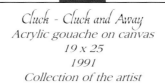

Cluck - Cluck and Away
Acrylic gouache on canvas
19 x 25
1991
Collection of the artist

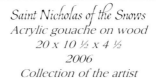

Saint Nicholas of the Snows
Acrylic gouache on wood
20 x 10 ½ x 4 ½
2006
Collection of the artist

Christmas Eve Journey
Acrylic gouache on tin
14 ¼ x 11 ½
2011
Collection of the artist

Lessons

"*There* are so many things that I still want to do and, as almost all decorative artists, I have many wood and metal pieces stashed to constantly tempt me; but, it is the wonderful artists who come to study with me that remain as my greatest inspiration. Helping me present decorative art over the years, these artists and their requests continually create in me the need to meet their requests and present historical studies for our enrichment and understanding. I want them to know and be proud of the rich, beautiful history of folk art, and the special love and need of painting pieces for family and friends that, to me, is the essence of folk art.

The nurse in me recognizes our need to have a special hobby to literally consume us. Winston Churchill told us that this type of hobby should be one that can be done almost to the end of our life. He also said that to squeeze out our colors onto the palette is 'delicious.'

As I look toward the new year, I'm already preparing pieces for class and some pieces for personal expression that I've been saving. It is now time to paint them and to prepare my palette – it will be delicious." — Jo Sonja

Hip Hop's Garden
Acrylic gouache on metal
2008
16 x 12 x 10
Collection of the artist

147

Damascened Fruit
Lesson on CD ROM

Webster's dictionary defines damascened as "to ornament with a wavy pattern." Damascened decoration may be on iron or steel as well as fabric (damask). Here the pattern is found on the floor of an old embossed tray. I have found that old trays are much better than newer ones because the embossing is usually deeper.

Any design may be painted with this soft, gentle "blushing" of color, so a flower design would be just as lovely as this fruit arrangement. Of course, this idea could also be painted on a plain surface, but don't you think this is a beautiful, unique look?

Penn Dutch Sampler
Lesson on CD ROM

Traditional decorative motifs are combined on this small sampler painting. The original inspiration was a small mirror by Peter Ompir, whose work became an inspiration for many of our early paintings in Oregon.

Here, I have painted a distlefink (a small thistle finch) "just for pretty," George and Martha Washington (an honored couple), and the ever-favorite strawberries motif.

Sharing a Life
Lesson on CD ROM

This plate is a tribute to my husband Jerry. It was painted during our celebration of 50 years of marriage. I can think of many occasions when this would make a special gift, so please enjoy! You can easily adapt this design to a variety of surfaces. Let your imagination soar!

Angelique Rose
Lesson on CD ROM

The color combinations on this piece perhaps draw your attention first. Then the softness of the very painterly style intrigues your eye and invites closer inspection. The mottled colors of the trim panels tie the floral panels together – truly a delightful combination.

Cherries Jubilee
Lesson on CD ROM

Celebrate delicious, colorful cherries! Here I use the cherry motif in a very traditionally inspired interpretation combining country tin painting techniques and design style. When combined with today's beautiful colors, elements of this design style yield a look that is truly refreshing.

Summer Medley
Lesson on CD ROM

Soft, cozy, witty — a very happy brush has been used to do this painting. Where do you find a happy brush? Well, you paint with your heart! Don't be logical about color, or think realistically about pattern. Be very painterly.

First Day of Christmas
Lesson on CD ROM

"*On* the first day of Christmas, my true love gave to me a partridge in a pear tree." This lovely old refrain was the inspiration for this design, which I hope brings much pleasure to you and your brush.

Songbird
Lesson on CD ROM

"*This* Bird Would Sing in Your Home"

This is a saying found on some Pennsylvania Dutch bird paintings and frakturs that were the inspiration for this study.

I have also included variegated stroke work for an interesting, contemporary addition to this beautiful old folk art form.

Hip Hop's Garden
Lesson on CD ROM

How about a tender red tulip or a succulent wild strawberry? Imagine the choices your painted garden presents Hip Hop! Enjoy painting him with his favorites.

Stroked Fruit
Lesson on CD ROM

Sometimes the most expressive, simple technique with basic colors can be so beautiful. Here is an example to illustrate that fact. These designs adapt easily to so many surfaces. Just imagine all the possibilities!

Instructional CD ROM

All of the instructions for painting the designs presented in the Lessons portion of this catalog are on the CD ROM located in the back of the book.

To use the CD, you must have Adobe Acrobat Reader installed on your computer. The program is on the disc if it is not already on your computer, and is compatible with boh PC and Mac formats.

Simply place the CD ROM into your computer's CD drive and the file should automatically open. If it does not, just click the file name to open.

All of the instructions, designs, and worksheets are included on the CD ROM. You may enlarge the images for easier viewing and you may print the designs for your personal use.

The CD ROM was designed to work on a computer; it will not play in a DVD player.

© 2011 National Museum of Decorative Painting - Used w

CHROMA

It's all about the paint.

In 1983, Chroma, Inc. joined forces with Jo Sonja Jansen to create a premier line of products for the discriminating decorative artist. With Jo Sonja's vision and guidance, the paints, mediums, and products that bear her name were created. Chroma's Jo Sonja products continue to evolve and inspire artists in countries around the world. The enduring relationship that was forged between us still continues to be strong nearly 30 years later.

We at Chroma are very pleased to have been partners with her for the development of this superb artists' quality product line and are equally proud to be a sponsor of *Jo Sonja –A Life In Folk Art*. This retrospective exhibition is a milestone in an unmatched, unprecedented career and we proudly salute her artistic achievements over the past 40 years of creativity.

Congratulations, Jo Sonja on this well deserved tribute to your life as a folk artist.

We cherish our partnership and look forward to many more years of continuing to develop, produce, and market your signature line of products to the finest artistic standards. We know your creative mind will, without a doubt, help us make the Chroma's Jo Sonja line of products the primary choice of artists who wish to create art of the highest caliber.

Bravo Jo Sonja on the retrospective exhibition and being designated a **Living Treasure!**

Sincerely,

Mark Kline, *Chroma Vice President*

And the entire Chroma family.